Somerset County Council

SCHOOL LIBRARY

BOOK NO. 233416   **CLASS** 553.7

Please return your books to the school library promptly after you have read them.

If you lose or damage a book you will be asked to pay for its replacement.

Water

The purpose of this book is to introduce you to the role water plays in our lives – to explain where it comes from; how it is used; why we cannot live without it; and to show the good and the bad that it can bring. With about two-thirds of the earth's surface covered with water, it plays a central part in all our lives and we all should know more about this, the most precious resource. Previously editor of *African Water and Sewage* and deputy editor of *Water Services* and *Middle East Water and Sewage*, Mark Corliss is currently the editor of *Asian Agribusiness*.

Focus on
WATER

Mark Corliss

Focus on Resources series

Alternative Energy
Coffee
Cotton
Dairy Produce
Gas
Grain
Nuclear Fuel
Oil
Seafood
Sugar
Tea
Timber
Water
Wool

Frontispiece *Irrigated paddy fields on the southern bank of the Yangtzi River in China.*

First published in 1985 by
Wayland (Publishers) Ltd
49 Lansdowne Place, Hove
East Sussex BN3 1HF, England

© Copyright 1985 Wayland (Publishers) Ltd

Phototypeset by Kalligraphics Ltd, Redhill, Surrey
Printed in Italy by G. Canale & C.S.p.A., Turin
Bound in Great Britain at The Bath Press, Avon

British Library Cataloguing in Publication Data

Corliss, Mark
  Focus on water. – (Focus on resources)
  1. Water – Juvenile literature
  I. Title   II. Series
  553.7   GB662.3

  ISBN 0–85078–602–9

Contents

1. What is water?

Water to most people is simply something which comes out of taps, falls as rain, flows in rivers or makes up the oceans. What is it, though?

Chemically, water is a combination of two hydrogen atoms and one oxygen atom, with the formula H_2O. It is one of the most interesting elements. It can be found either as a solid (ice), a liquid, or a gas (steam), and can be changed from one to the other quite easily. Very rarely, though, can it be found in its pure form of H_2O because other substances have usually been dissolved in it. An example of this is sea water, which can contain a very high proportion of salt, making it totally undrinkable.

Unlike most substances, when water becomes solid – that is when its temperature drops below $0^{\circ}C$ and it forms ice – it actually expands rather than contracting. If you were to

Most of us take water for granted. It is always there — at the turn of a tap. But where does it come from?

leave a bottle full of water in a freezer or outside on a day when the temperature dropped to below freezing point, the water would solidify and, as it was held in by the sides of the bottle, it would slowly push its way up the neck to form a thin 'plug' of ice coming out of the top.

Water also expands when it is heated up, but the effects of this are not so noticeable until it reaches its boiling point – 100°C – when it will become a gas.

The Baltoro Glacier in the Karakoram Mountains of Pakistan. A glacier is a river of frozen water.

2. The hydrological cycle

Every day, all over the world, millions of gallons of water are used in houses, factories, offices and shops. Where does it come from and why does it not run out? The answer lies in something called the hydrological cycle, which is also called the water cycle.

Water on the earth's surface – in rivers, lakes and the sea – is evaporated by the sun's rays and rises above the earth until it cools and forms into droplets. These absorb small particles of dust to form clouds.

Carried by air currents, these clouds are blown across the sky and as they cool, so the droplets become larger and heavier and fall back to the earth as rain.

In some areas of the world, especially in the

The movement of water from the world's oceans to the atmosphere and back again is known as the hydrological cycle.

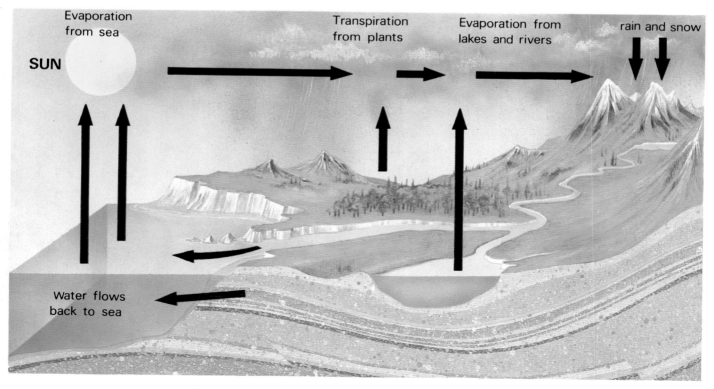

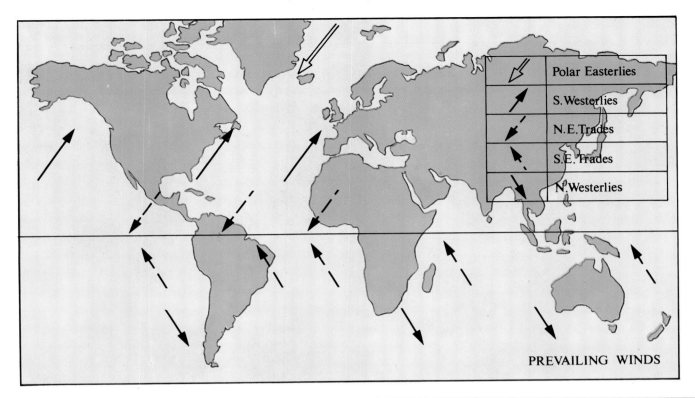

⬊	Polar Easterlies
⬈	S. Westerlies
⬊	N.E. Trades
⬈	S.E. Trades
⬊	N. Westerlies

PREVAILING WINDS

Water-bearing clouds are blown across our skies by the prevailing winds.

extreme north and south, the air temperature at cloud level is very cold and the water droplets turn to crystals of ice. As these get heavier and fall to earth, the temperature may not rise above freezing point and the crystals, now recognizable as snow, settle on the earth's surface.

However the water returns to earth, the pattern of the hydrological cycle never changes. Water evaporates, falls to the ground and runs into rivers and lakes and then on to the sea in a continuous process of evaporation, cooling and precipitation (the term for water that falls as rain, snow or hail).

The snowy, icy landscape of the North Pole.

3. Sources of water

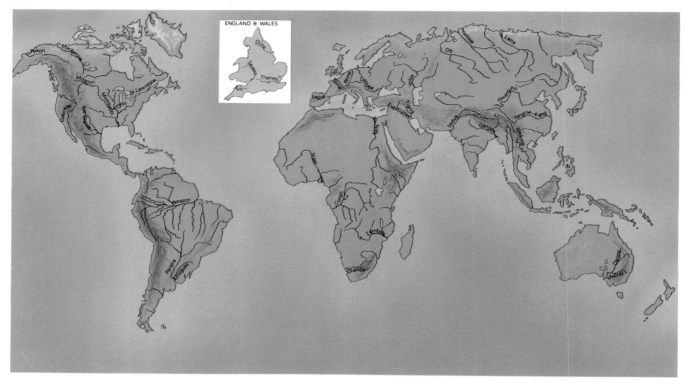

The main rivers of the world. Only about 3 per cent of the earth's water is in its rivers and lakes.

We have just examined how water is naturally moved around the world, so now let us look at where it exists on the earth's surface. To start with, there is the ground underneath us.

Under almost all land lie water-bearing rocks which contain water in either small pockets or in vast reservoirs. These resources, known as aquifers, are thought to contain 5,000 million million cubic metres of water within the top three-quarters of a kilometre of the earth's crust (one cubic metre is the equivalent of 1,000 litres or 220 gallons). Much of this water is

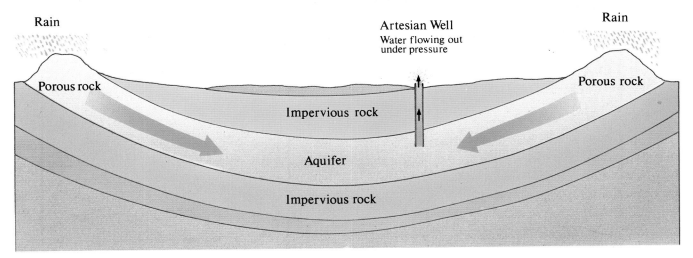

Rain

Artesian Well
Water flowing out under pressure

Rain

Porous rock

Impervious rock

Aquifer

Impervious rock

Porous rock

either of very poor quality or inaccessible, so we must rely on the reserves on the surface to provide us with most of our daily requirements.

About 65 per cent of the earth's surface is covered by water and nearly all of this is in the oceans. Only about 3 per cent is in rivers and lakes. When you imagine the size of some of these — rivers such as the Amazon, Mississippi, Nile, Ganges, Indus and the Volga and lakes such as the Great Lakes, Kariba, Victoria and Bratsk (in Russia) — it puts the total quantity of water into perspective.

A cross-section of an aquifer.

In addition to this, but representing a smaller proportion of the total available, is the water kept permanently in the form of snow and ice which exists at the North and South Poles, in icebergs and glaciers and on the top of the world's many high mountain ranges.

There is an enormous aquifer under London in the chalk (light areas).

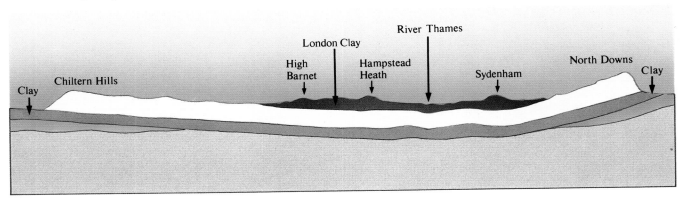

London Clay

River Thames

High Barnet

Hampstead Heath

North Downs

Chiltern Hills

Sydenham

Clay

Clay

4. The demand for water

Obviously not all the water on the earth is available for us to use, so man is limited to using that which is easily accessible. New methods of obtaining water are constantly being investigated, but since the time of the Industrial Revolution in the nineteenth century, it is true to say that as mankind becomes more sophisticated, the thirstier he seems to grow.

In developed countries, recent statistics show that the daily consumption of water can be as high as 150 litres (33 gallons) per person – more if the water used by industry is included. In contrast, many of the developing countries have a daily requirement of only about 12 litres (2.5 gallons) per person, particularly in the rural areas.

It is not hard to explain this contrast. Countries, such as the USA, Australia and the Western European nations, are now highly industrialized and this creates a demand for water for cleaning

Washing machines and dishwashers all increase the demand for water in the developed nations.

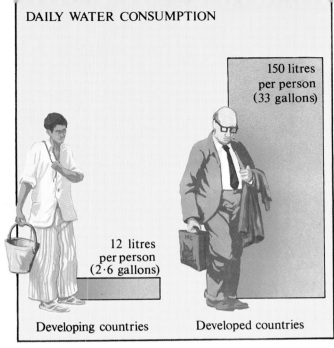

DAILY WATER CONSUMPTION

150 litres
per person
(33 gallons)

12 litres
per person
(2·6 gallons)

Developing countries   Developed countries

People in the developed nations consume more than ten times the amount of water consumed in developing countries.

or for cooking. Most families in these countries have washing machines and many have dishwashers in their houses. These countries also have higher standards of hygiene which call for flush toilets and regular baths. And we all want to be able to drink as much as we want.

In developing countries, on the other hand, industry is not so widespread; washing and cleaning are not undertaken so frequently; and not having a regular, piped water supply prevents many people from being so wasteful of what is, after all, a precious commodity.

Below   *Having to queue for their water and then carry it home means that people in developing nations do not waste it.*

5. Water in developed countries

The Romans were the first to recognize the importance of providing an adequate water supply to their towns and were responsible for building aqueducts and public bath houses. They also introduced the first basic sewers.

With the fall of the Roman Empire in the fifth century AD, many of these advances were forgotten and we must jump ahead to the eighteenth and nineteenth centuries before any further progress was made in the control of water supplies. Early towns and villages relied

Below *An aqueduct built by the Romans in southern France.*

In many parts of Britain, water used to be delivered by horse and cart.

on wells for their drinking water but, during the Industrial Revolution, these proved inadequate to cope with the increased demand.

So the great engineers of the time turned their attention to solving the problems of bringing good quality water to meet this demand. Big storage reservoirs were formed in upland regions to store river and rainwater and long pipelines were constructed, usually of cast iron, to carry this water to where it was needed.

Other developments, such as the steam-engine and the modern water wheel, allowed greater quantities of water to be pumped or distributed over long distances. New laws were also passed to control the quality and availability of water.

Most industrialized countries now use and re-use their water supplies to gain the maximum benefit from them. Water from rivers, reservoirs or aquifers, is treated to make it drinkable and dirty water is discharged to the sewers.

Most houses and factories have an inlet for clean water — the mains supply — and an outlet for waste, or used, water — the sewer. Water in the sewers flows to a waste water (or sewage) treatment works where it is processed and discharged back into the main source of supply, normally a river.

Water from the River Thames, for example, is re-used up to seven times as it flows through London. This does not mean that the water supplied to houses in London is ever dirty because each time the water is taken from the Thames, it is treated and purified before being put into the water mains and used by families and industry.

This diagram shows how water is piped into, around, and removed from a house.

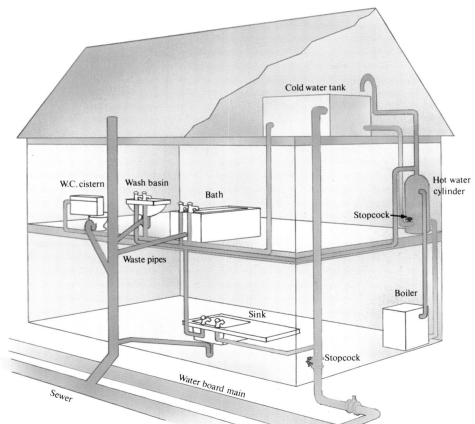

15

6. Water in developing countries

Developing countries do not have the money to build the types of comprehensive water supply systems that exist in most developed nations.

Current statistics from the United Nations show that of the 1.8 million people living in the

In many developing countries, wells are the main source of people's water. This is a well in a Pakistani village.

A water-treatment plant near Nairobi, in Kenya.

rural areas of developing countries, only 1 in 5 has access to a reliable source of clean water. The remainder have to make do with untreated river water, rainwater or unreliable wells for their daily requirements – and often have to go without water for washing and cooking.

But most of the major cities in developing countries now have modern water-treatment plants linked to a reliable source of water, often some distance away and connected by major pipelines. In the rural areas, too, help is coming and villagers are being instructed in health care, hygiene and very simple water-treatment techniques, such as boiling or filtering through charcoal. The villagers are also being taught how to use and maintain handpumps to allow them to draw water from greater depths, often from locations closer to their homes.

Since water is not piped to their homes, many people in developing countries have to use nearby rivers for their washing and as a source of water.

7. Drought – its impact

Ethiopians queuing for food and water in 1984. It has not rained there for several years.

Despite the apparent abundance of water throughout the world, most people rely on rainfall – the final product of the hydrological cycle – for their daily water supply.

Most areas of the world have variable rainfall patterns and many have a distinguishable rainy and dry season. It is when these patterns change, either permanently or temporarily, that the problems of drought start to occur.

The effects of drought, though, are often far more long-term than the actual period when rain does not fall. If the water is not available at

The drought in 1976 lowered the water level in most of the reservoirs in Britain.

mercy of changing weather patterns, have had no proper rainfall for several years.

The answers are never clear in extreme cases such as these, because simply spending more money on new water-supply schemes is not always the solution. Later in the book we will look at some of the steps being taken to ease the situation in the worst affected areas, but the fact remains that the drastic change in life style for the hundreds of thousands of people involved will remain for some time.

This Indian dam controls the water supply in times of flood and low rainfall.

the time when crops are growing, for example, a complete season can be lost. Also if the rains come at the wrong time, valuable topsoil can be washed away, bringing even more severe problems to the vast areas dependent on agriculture for their livelihood.

This problem has been highlighted in recent years in India and in the area known as the Sahel, which runs in a broad belt across North Africa. In 1984 world attention was focused on Ethiopia and the Sudan, two countries totally dependent on agriculture and which, at the

8. Purifying water

The water that we can obtain for drinking is rarely pure and usually has to be treated before it is drinkable.

Water in rivers, in reservoirs and in underground aquifers can easily become polluted by industrial waste, sewage, the drainage of fertilizers and other agricultural chemicals from farmers' fields or, more simply, from the rocks and soil through which it flows. Over the centuries, therefore, methods of treating water to reduce or eliminate harmful substances have evolved: the most simple being to boil the water and allow it to cool before drinking.

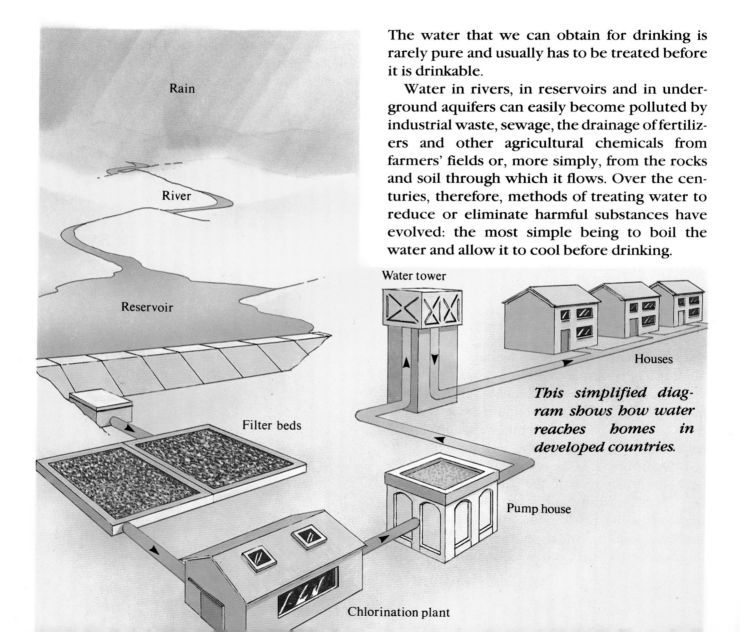

Rain

River

Reservoir

Water tower

Houses

This simplified diagram shows how water reaches homes in developed countries.

Filter beds

Pump house

Chlorination plant

Modern water-treatment works, often located on or near a major river or reservoir, use complicated equipment and chemicals to perform what is basically a very simple operation: to 'scrub' the water and remove unwanted particles or bacteria.

The simplest method of purifying water involves passing it first through a combination of screens and strainers; then through sedimentation tanks to allow particles to settle to the bottom; the next stage is 'coagulation', where chemicals are added to bond the remaining tiny particles together, making them heavier and allowing these, too, to settle; after this the water is filtered through beds of sand; the final process is the addition of chemicals to kill off any remaining bacteria. The chemicals used for this vary according to the practice of individual countries or areas, but they are usually chlorine or ozone. These destroy the harmful germs immediately and also remain in the water, providing some protection while it is in the pipes being distributed to homes, schools, factories or farms.

These water-storage towers in the Middle East are attractive architectural features.

9. Pollution and disease

Wherever there is a source of water, it can be polluted from a number of sources. These are usually connected with the discharge of industrial or domestic waste water into rivers or aquifers — either accidentally or intentionally — which can result in serious outbreaks of disease.

In major cities, most water for drinking is treated using the methods described in the previous chapter, so it is usually in rural areas where the main dangers lie.

Untreated sewage or the water draining off agricultural land or even a mass of falling leaves can 'kill' a river by using up all its oxygen, poisoning the water and leading to the death of fish and plant life. In addition, many diseases such as cholera, typhoid, dysentery and bilharzia (or 'snail fever', caused by a parasite which lives in freshwater snails) exist in many of the

Agricultural chemicals can drain off the land and poison nearby rivers. This helicopter is spraying weedkiller over land in New Zealand.

rivers and lakes regularly used for bathing, drinking or cooking in developing countries.

The effects of such disease are largely under control in developed countries, which have introduced laws about the standards of cleanliness and purity of the water we are to drink. The problems remain very great in the rest of the world and have a serious effect on peoples' ability to carry out their daily lives or to perform their jobs.

The World Health Organization claims that 80 per cent of all sickness and disease in the world is caused by inadequate clean water supplies and the lack of proper sanitation facilities.

Lime being dropped into a Swedish lake to reduce its water's acidity.

Above *Industrial pollution in the River Athi downstream from Nairobi, Kenya.*

10. Sewage treatment

Like the treatment of water in developed countries prior to its supply to households, there are strict regulations about how the used, dirty water is disposed of.

Most modern houses and factories are connected to pipelines (known as sewers) which carry this dirty water away. At the end of the sewer lies the sewage-treatment works. These are normally situated by a river or the sea, into which the treated water is discharged.

At the entrance to a modern sewage works, the water is screened to remove coarse material and the remaining liquid flows through a network of tanks and filters before it is considered clean enough to be discharged.

A modern sewage-treatment plant.

The first stage in the process is known as 'primary sedimentation'. Here, the dirty water flows into large tanks and the small particles in it settle to the bottom to form a sludge, which is then scraped away. In contrast with drinking-water treatment, most waste-water treatment systems rely on biological action for their effectiveness. Naturally occurring bacteria exist in the next phase, the 'contact beds', in which the water is sprayed on to the top of a tank containing coarse stones or plastic 'media'. These bacteria form a layer on the surface of this 'media' and biologically break down the waste matter.

After this, the water is passed to a further tank where, again, any remaining solids are allowed to settle out. At this stage the water may be clear enough to be discharged but in some situations where the water is to be re-used, it will go through a third stage.

This involves a similar process to that used for drinking-water treatment and makes use of very fine screens or strainers, or passing it through deep beds of sand.

This diagram shows how waste from homes and factories is treated at a modern sewage works. Waste water is treated so that it can be returned to a river. Solid waste is treated so that it can either be re-used in agriculture (removed by road tanker) or dumped at sea.

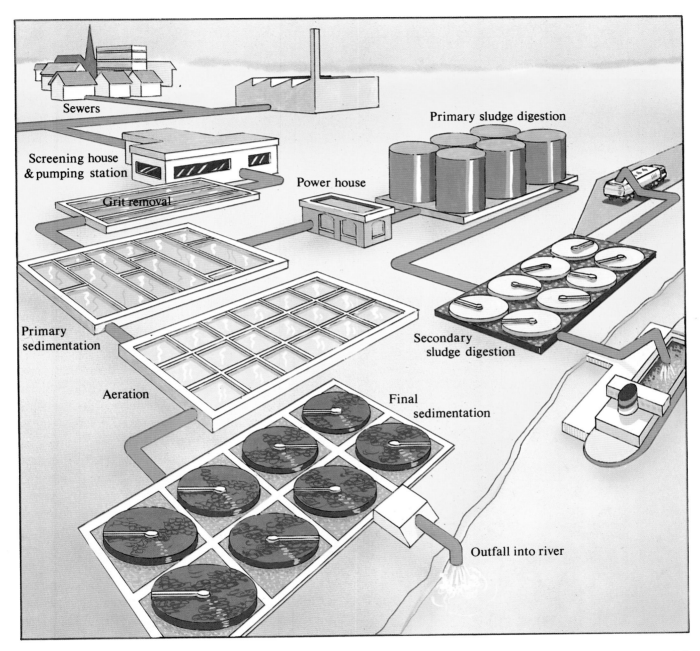

Sewers

Screening house
& pumping station

Grit removal

Primary sludge digestion

Power house

Primary
sedimentation

Secondary
sludge digestion

Aeration

Final
sedimentation

Outfall into river

25

11. Water distribution

From about the beginning of the seventeenth century, water distribution systems were made of wooden pipes, made from tree trunks. In fact, this practice still continues in some countries, with hollowed-out bamboo being used.

The problem of making large-diameter water

An ambitious project to create a huge lake in the Rockies to supply both California and Mexico.

pipes was not solved until the end of the eighteenth century, when the cast-iron pipe, together with the water-tight joint, were invented in Britain. Today most water pipes are made of reinforced concrete.

Water to be supplied to the consumer flows from the treatment works in trunk mains (another name for pipes) to a service reservoir or a water tower which will serve a relatively small area. To obtain the required pressure for the user, water is then distributed through smaller, pressure mains which divide to form service mains through which individual houses are served.

The local distribution of domestic and industrial water supplies is usually done under low pressure in piped systems; while the bulk transfer of water from one area to another is more commonly by gravity flow.

Probably the best example of the bulk transfer of water is the Snowy Mountain scheme in Australia. This is designed to transfer water from the Snowy River, which flows through well-watered land, across the Great Dividing Range into the Murray River to supply an area regularly short of water. Over 130 km (93 miles) of aqueducts are involved, some of which are tunnels about 7 metres (23 feet) in diameter. The scheme also provides electricity from 11 hydroelectric power stations.

Above *In the Philippines, these bamboo pipes bring water from a nearby spring to a village.*
Below *This impressive dam is part of the Snowy River water transfer scheme in Australia.*

12. Water for transport

From the earliest days, man has realized that water was an efficient and simple way to move both people and produce from one place to another.

Of course, at the beginning, boat-building methods were very simple, often involving hollowing out a tree trunk, and the distances travelled were very short. As time went by, better and bigger boats were built, allowing people to go to new lands far away, in search of new sources of food or greater wealth.

History shows that people have travelled from Ireland to North America, from Scandinavia to Britain, and all over the Pacific in very small man-powered crafts. Later, other forms of power were harnessed — allowing greater distances to be covered reliably and opening up trade with the far corners of the globe.

The main shipping routes are shown on this map. The thicker the line, the more goods are carried on the route.

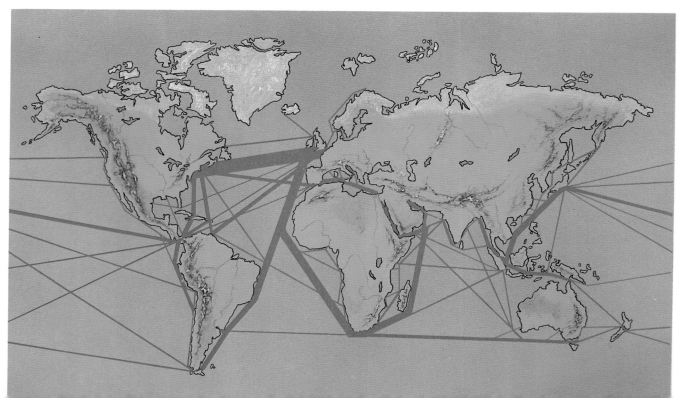

Every day, hundreds of barges carry goods up and down the River Rhine and the canals linked to it.

Today, almost all materials to be sent from one country to another, not linked by road or rail, are sent by sea. Also, many countries have developed their river networks, sometimes by linking them with canals, to allow a cheap form of transport from one town to another. The River Rhine, which flows through Switzerland and Germany before reaching the sea in the Netherlands, is a perfect example of this and every day hundreds of barges carrying goods can be seen ploughing their way along the river.

Busy, bustling Piraeus harbour, near Athens. It is the heart of the Greek shipping industry.

13. Water for energy

The energy in moving water has been used for centuries to provide power, initially for grinding corn or driving very simple forms of pump.

By the nineteenth century, engineers had designed highly efficient water wheels which, with the help of a system of gears, could be used to power machines in factories.

Nowadays, a modern version of the water wheel, the water turbine, is used in many countries to generate electricity – a method known as hydroelectric power: fast-flowing water spins turbines which drive electromagnets to generate electricity. Usually this method harnesses the power of water in fast-flowing rivers

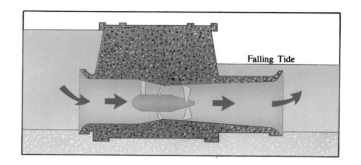

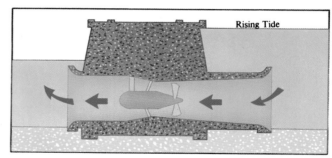

Above *A cross-section of the dam across the River Rance's estuary in northern France. The rising and falling tides spin turbines which power generators to produce electricity.*

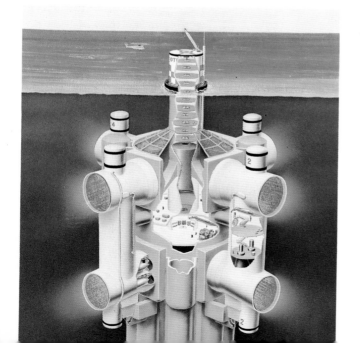

Left *Giant floats, like this, are going to be used to generate electricity. They make use of the fact that in most oceans water at the surface is hotter than deeper down.*

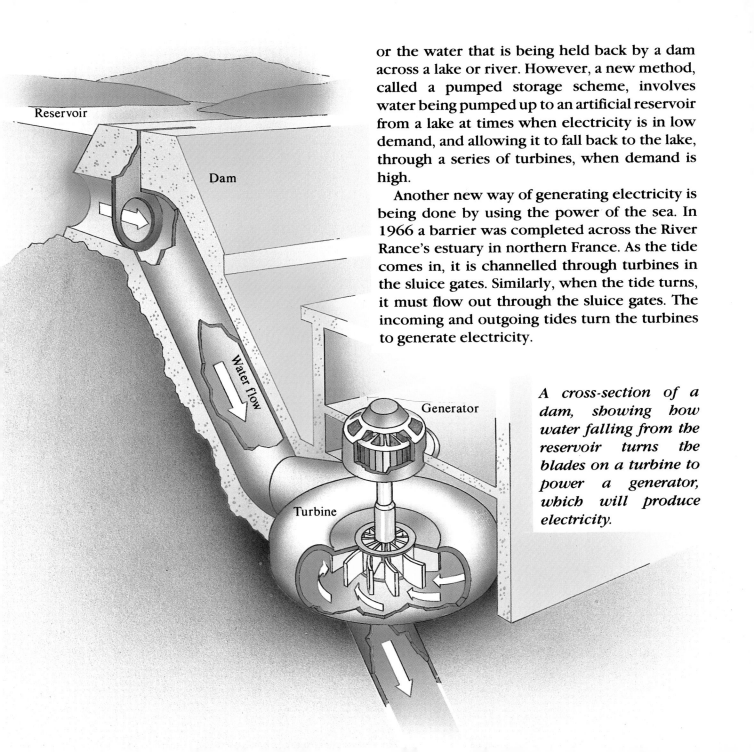

Reservoir

Dam

Water flow

Generator

Turbine

or the water that is being held back by a dam across a lake or river. However, a new method, called a pumped storage scheme, involves water being pumped up to an artificial reservoir from a lake at times when electricity is in low demand, and allowing it to fall back to the lake, through a series of turbines, when demand is high.

Another new way of generating electricity is being done by using the power of the sea. In 1966 a barrier was completed across the River Rance's estuary in northern France. As the tide comes in, it is channelled through turbines in the sluice gates. Similarly, when the tide turns, it must flow out through the sluice gates. The incoming and outgoing tides turn the turbines to generate electricity.

A cross-section of a dam, showing how water falling from the reservoir turns the blades on a turbine to power a generator, which will produce electricity.

14. Water for agriculture

A rice paddy field in Japan. Rice needs 4,500 kilograms of water to grow just one kilogram of it.

Although a lot of water is used in houses and industry, much, much more is used in agriculture. About 1,250 million hectares (3,100 million acres) of land are under cultivation, representing almost 10 per cent of the world's land; and of this, one per cent is irrigated or artificially provided with water. The remaining land is watered by rainfall.

All plants need water to grow and all livestock and human beings must have water to survive. The biggest single crop grown in the world is rice. Most of it is produced in Asia. Rice requires 4,500 kilograms of water to grow just one kilogram of the crop. To put this into perspective, wheat needs just 1,500 kilograms of water; while cotton requires a massive

These irrigation channels supply river water to fields in the Gambia, western Africa.

10,000 kilograms.

Water, therefore, is essential for agricultural production. Farmers must conserve the rain and channel it into their fields in the right quantities and at the right time. Most irrigation systems involve a network of canals and ditches connected to the fields, but separated by sluice gates to control the distribution of the water.

More complicated methods involve sprinkler systems moving over the crop, spraying a precise quantity of water over a given area; or 'drip' systems, made of small plastic pipes, which drip water at the base of the plant, allowing it to go straight to the roots, so avoiding unwanted evaporation.

Below *Overhead water sprayers in action on a farm in France.*

15. Water for industry

Industry uses large amounts of water for cooling, for washing products and even for making some products – especially drinks and some foods. But how and where is it actually used?

Power stations probably require the greatest amount of water, mainly for cooling. When a power station is in operation, enormous amounts of heat are produced. Elaborate cooling systems have to be installed to prevent its

Power stations need a lot of water for cooling.

Some 450,000 litres (99,000 gallons) of water are needed to make a typical car.

machinery burning up. The water discharged from these places is obviously very hot and so it can be used in other areas, either on the same site or, via underground pipes, to heat houses and factories nearby – a system popular in many parts of Europe.

Such products as mineral ores – iron, copper, and coal, for example – need to be washed before industry can make use of them. The end-

34

products of industrial production, such as paper and steel, also need to be washed or cooled before they can be distributed from the factory.

As water becomes more expensive, many factories have installed waste-water recycling facilities so that they can use the same water time and time again, only topping up the level as necessary. This operation is also valuable to companies in another way, as the used water often contains re-usable waste products. For example, a factory which applies silver plate to cutlery would recycle its waste-water and, using a specially designed collection device, reclaim some of the silver which had not been used the first time around.

(1) The heat in a power station's cooling water is lost to the atmosphere when it is cooled. (2) The hot water, along with similar water from factories and refuse-burning plants, could be used to heat local homes and industries.

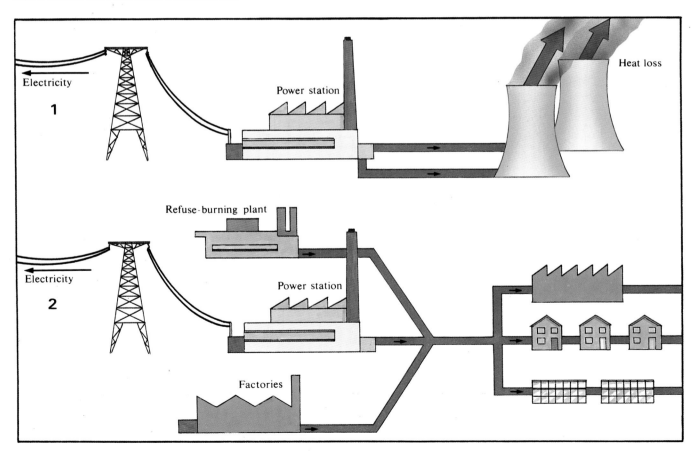

16. Water and recreation

More people are estimated to spend their leisure time in a pursuit connected with water — sailing, swimming, and fishing, for example — than in any other activity.

This is becoming more and more the case as our leisure time increases with the introduction of modern technology. This fact is acknowledged by local government authorities and the other organizations responsible for the provision of recreational facilities, and in the last 15 to 20 years there has been a dramatic increase

The marina in Auckland, New Zealand.

Skiing is becoming an increasingly popular outdoor activity.

in the availability of such outlets. New swimming pools and ice-skating rinks are opening; sailing, rowing and canoeing clubs are expanding; and more and more people are getting used to thinking of water as a source of enjoyment.

And these leisure activities are not confined to what most would think of as warm weather sports. Skiing is becoming increasingly popular, as are outdoor ice skating, ice hockey and tobogganing — all of which involve water in its solid form: snow or ice.

A party of people shooting the rapids on the River Ottawa in Canada.

17. Desalination

In many countries, water is not available from rivers or rainfall, so people have to turn to the sea or contaminated underground sources for their supplies.

Recent technological advances have made this process much easier and desalination – literally removing salts from water – is a very real alternative. Like most highly complex processes however, it is expensive, so it is fortunate that those countries that require it most are wealthy enough to pay for it. It is a process mostly used in the Middle East.

There are three main methods for removing salts from water: reverse osmosis, distillation and electrodialysis. Reverse osmosis involves passing the water under pressure through a membrane which allows pure water to flow through it but which retains the salts. Distilla-

An aerial view of a sewage-treatment plant under construction in the Middle East. It can purify dirty water so that it can be re-used.

Drilling for new supplies of fresh water in the Middle East.

tion uses extreme heat to turn the pure water into steam, leaving the salt behind as a residue; while electrodialysis uses an electro-chemical process, in conjunction with filters and membranes, to separate pure water out from the solution.

Because of the enormous power requirements of the distillation process, and the heat generated as a by-product, this system is often linked with another industrial activity. An example of this is the large aluminium smelter in Dubai in the United Arab Emirates. Aluminium requires enormous amounts of heat to melt and process the ore and the Dubai Aluminium Company built its plant with the intention of selling the good quality water it produced to the nearby city to subsidize its aluminium production.

Below *The desalination plant of the Dubai Aluminium Company.*

18. The Water Decade

In many developing countries, a poor water supply and an unsatisfactory waste-disposal system sustain a vicious circle of poverty, disease, low industrial productivity and a high death rate among babies and children.

To try to break this vicious circle, which affects millions of people around the world, the United Nations held a special conference in 1977. The delegates to this conference proposed an International Drinking Water and Sanitation Decade to run from 1981 to 1990 and this was later approved by the United Nations General Assembly.

Better known as the Water Decade, its aim is to bring clean drinking water and basic sanitation facilities to all the world's population. According to the World Health Organization, which is helping to co-ordinate the Decade, this would involve reaching 1.8 *billion* people with clean water and 2.4 *billion* with sanitation.

This is obviously a massive task and one that requires great dedication on the part of all the organizations involved. To improve the water supply and sanitation facilities in rural areas involves not only finding new sources of water but also introducing cheaper and more effective ways of distributing this water. One big problem remains: according to most experts involved with the Decade, the biggest obstacle

It is hoped that by 1990 the majority of water-borne diseases will have been eliminated.

Above *While half the world lacks clean water, the other half uses it to clean cars.*

Below *The Water Decade aims to bring clean drinking water to everyone.*

is not a lack of funds, but the lack of trained people within organizations capable of carrying out what needs to be done in the developing nations.

Despite this, considerable progress has been made. While the Decade's full aims are unlikely ever to be reached, the attention drawn to this problem has encouraged many people to become involved and bring benefits to the needy. One of the organizations involved in the Decade, the United Nations Children's Fund, helped bring some 13 million people their first regular supplies of clean water in 1983.

19. The future

There is an enormous amount of water on this planet, as we have seen, but only a small amount is available for our use. As a result of improved living standards, greater demands from agriculture and an ever-increasing world population, scientists are examining ways of making more of this precious, unobtainable liquid available.

We have already seen how it is possible to obtain pure water from the sea and to re-use polluted water, but more adventurous ideas have been put forward to increase the supply still further. In some highly industrialized countries, 'conjunctive use' schemes are being constructed whereby rivers are linked by tunnel or pipelines to transfer water from one area to another. This allows the water to be demanded in one area and supplied from another which is probably some distance away and separated by a natural barrier such as a mountain.

In the oil-rich countries of the Middle East two more ideas are being examined, which are more far-fetched but theoretically possible.

One ambitious proposal is to tow icebergs from the Antarctic to the Middle East and allow them to melt inside special containers.

'Seeding' clouds to encourage rain.

One is to tow an iceberg from the Antarctic to one of the Arabian countries and allow it to melt inside specially constructed structures. Another idea, currently being tested by Middle Eastern countries, is to send oil tankers to countries which not only want oil, but also have water available to exchange for it. The tankers discharge their load of oil and then load up with fresh water which is taken in part payment for the oil. Japan and Britain are two countries with ample water supplies to undertake this adventurous scheme and early results have been encouraging.

More scientific methods are also being car-ried out, such as reversing the flow of rivers with sophisticated pumps to bring water to where it is most needed. This is currently being tried out in the USSR and South Africa.

Equally futuristic, but much harder to achieve, is the 'seeding' of clouds to make them rain at a specific time and place. American and Israeli scientists have experimented with this option for many years, with differing levels of success, but the implications of such projects are vast.

Facts and figures

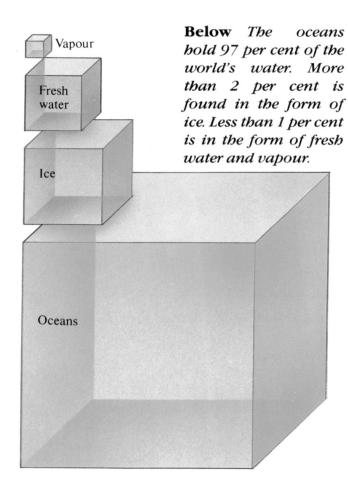

Vapour

Fresh water

Ice

Oceans

Below *The oceans hold 97 per cent of the world's water. More than 2 per cent is found in the form of ice. Less than 1 per cent is in the form of fresh water and vapour.*

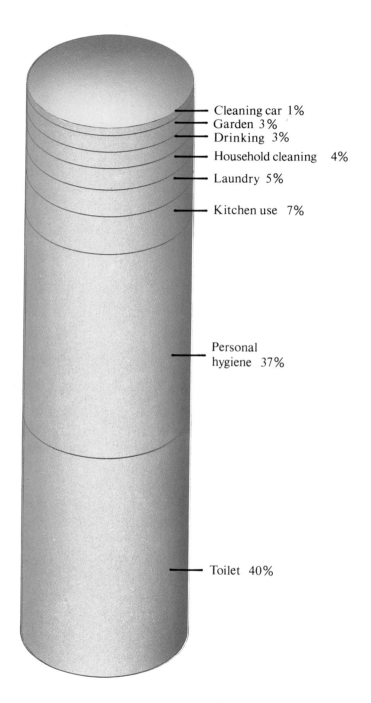

Cleaning car 1%
Garden 3%
Drinking 3%
Household cleaning 4%
Laundry 5%
Kitchen use 7%

Personal hygiene 37%

Toilet 40%

Right *This diagram shows how water is used in a typical home in a developed country.*

Water consumption

Daily water consumption per person in developing countries:

	Litres	Gallons
Africa	15–35	3.3–7.7
Southeast Asia	30–70	6.6–15.4
Western Pacific	30–95	6.6–21.0
Eastern Mediterranean	40–85	9.0–19.0
Algeria, Morocco & Turkey	20–65	4.4–14.3
Latin America & Caribbean	70–190	15.4–42.0
Average for all developing countries:	35–90	7.7–19.8
(Western Europe & North America:	100–270	22.0–59.3)
City people dependent on standpipes	10–15	2.2–3.3
City people with a single household tap	15–120	3.3–26.4
City people with several taps	30–300	6.6–66.0
Villagers without taps or standpipes	4–25	1–5.5
Villagers with standpipes or domestic taps	15–120	3.3–26.4

(A daily consumption of 5 litres (1.1 gallons) is considered to be the minimum amount necessary to sustain a person's basic needs)

The average daily consumption of water in a large modern city is sometimes as much as 2,000 litres (440 gallons) per person. This includes industrial, commericial and domestic consumption. A more typical figure for the average city is 500 litres (110 gallons) per person per day.

(Figures supplied by the World Health Organization)

Glossary

Aqueduct A man-made bridge with a channel for transporting water across a valley.

Aquifer A layer of rocks beneath the earth's surface containing water, which has seeped down from the surface, that can be used to supply wells.

Bacteria Microscopic creatures, some of them harmful, which live everywhere, including in and on the human body.

Biological action The use of naturally occurring bacteria in water or sewage to break down the waste material, rather than using artificial means, such as chemicals.

Coagulation Changing a liquid into a semi-solid mass by the addition of chemicals.

Contact beds The tanks in a sewage-treatment plant where biological action takes place.

Desalination The removal of salts from water, to make it fit for human consumption.

Distillation To purify a liquid by turning it first into a vapour, by means of heat, and then turning the vapour back into a liquid, by cooling it.

Electrodialysis The removal of solid particles from a liquid by attracting them to an electrode inserted in the liquid.

Evaporation The process by which water turns into vapour.

Filtration The straining of a liquid to remove any solid particles floating in it.

Hydroelectricity Electricity generated by the pressure of falling water.

Hydrological cycle The circulation of the earth's water: it evaporates from the sea into the atmosphere, falls to the earth as rain or snow, and returns to the sea in rivers, or to the atmosphere by evaporation.

Irrigation To supply areas of land with water using artificial canals or ditches to provide crops with water that they might not otherwise receive.

Membrane A very thin, flexible material that acts like a strainer to separate solid particles out of a liquid.

Precipitation The rain, snow, sleet and hail formed by the condensation of water vapour in the earth's atmosphere.

Reverse osmosis The filtering of a liquid by forcing it through a membrane under pressure.

Sanitation The conditions we try to create to keep ourselves and society free from dirt, infections and things harmful to our health. Good drainage systems, the efficient disposal of waste, and high standards of hygiene, all contribute to healthy living.

Sedimentation Allowing sludge to settle out of dirty water.

Service mains The water pipes which take water from trunk mains to houses, shops and factories.

Service reservoir A small storage tank containing clean water ready for distribution to industries and homes.

Trunk mains The large water pipes which bring water into another supply area.

Undeveloped countries The 'poorer' nations of the world which lack the resources (both in terms of money and manpower) to advance. They are still mainly agricultural, have little manufacturing industries, and have poor facilities.

Vapour The invisible, gas-like form of a substance that is usually a liquid or solid.

Waste water The water which has been dirtied in some way and which needs to be treated.

Books to read

CARPI, P. (editor) *The Book of Water* (Benn, 1980)
CATHERALL, E. *Water Power* (Wayland, 1981)
FOX, J. *The Water from your Tap* (Wayland, 1982)
GUNSTON, B. *Water* (Macdonald Educational, 1980)
JENNINGS, T. *Water* (Oxford University Press, 1982)
LEWIS, A. *Water* (Franklin Watts, 1980)
PAYNE, S. N. *Wind and Water Energy* (Blackwell Raintree, 1983)
READ, B. *The Water We Used* (World's Work, The Windmill Press, 1972)
SOWRY, J. *Looking at Water* (Batsford, 1982)

Picture acknowledgements

The author and publishers would like to thank the following for allowing their illustrations to be reproduced in this book: The Australian Information Service, London 27 (bottom); Camerapix Hutchison Library 13 (bottom), 16, 17 (Leslie Woodhead), 18; Edward Carr 6; Central Electricity Generating Board 34 (bottom); B.D. Hamilton (14 bottom), Bruce Coleman (19 top), Peter Davey (23 top), M. Timothy O'Keefe (24), Mark Boulton (33 top), A.J. Deane (33 bottom), Colin Molyneux (41 top) — all from Bruce Coleman Ltd; Mark Corliss 16 (top), 21, 39 (bottom); Bill Donohoe 8, 9 (top), 10, 26, 28; Drilltech 39 (top); Ford Motor Co. 34 (top); Lockheed Missiles and Space Co. 30 (bottom); Simon-Hartley Ltd 38; The Swedish NGO Secretariat on Acid Rain 23 (bottom; © Christer Agren); Malcolm Walker 11 (both), 13 (top), 15, 20, 25, 30 (top), 31, 35, 42, 43; Wayland Picture Library *cover*, 7, 9 (bottom), 12, 14 (top), 19 (bottom), 22, 29 (bottom), 29 (top), 32, 36 (both), 37; World Health Organization 27 (top), 40, 41 (bottom); Xinhua News Agency *frontispiece*.

Index